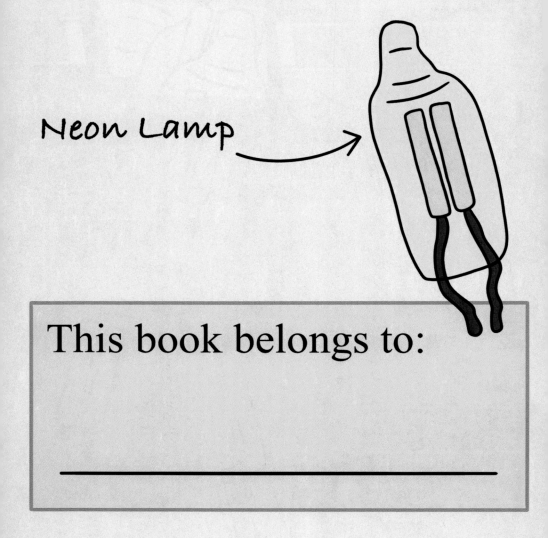

Neon Lamp

This book belongs to:

_____

Radio

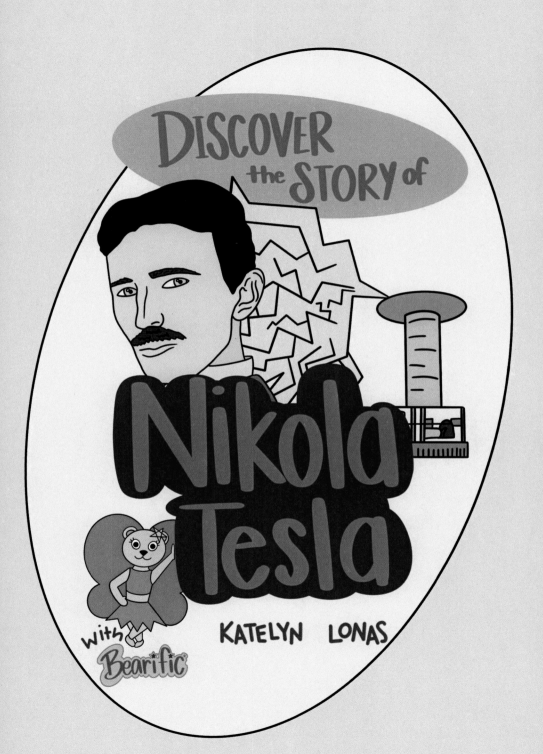

DISCOVER the STORY of

Nikola Tesla

with Bearific

KATELYN LONAS

Table of Contents

Early Life

Smiljan, Croatia

Nikola Tesla was raised in Smiljan, Croatia. His father Milutin Tesla was a Serbian orthodox priest and a writer.

Growing up Milutin pushed for Nikola to join the priesthood, but Nikola was always interested in science.

Milutin Tesla

Đuka Tesla

Nikola Tesla's interest in electrical inventions were inspired by his mother Ðuka Tesla, who often invented small household appliances in her spare time.

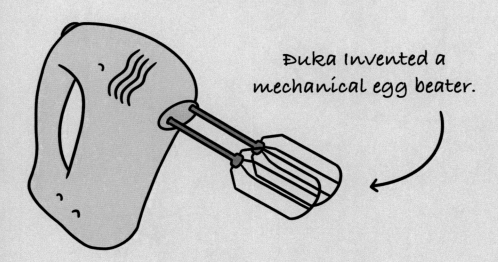

Ðuka Invented a mechanical egg beater.

He had four other siblings named Dane, Angelina, Milka and Marica.

Milka Tesla

Angelina Tesla

Marica Tesla

Dane Tesla

Education

Nikola Tesla finished high school in three years.

He first studied alternating currents and electrical engineering at Austrian Polytechnic in Graz, but left in his third year and did not receive a degree.

Tesla vs Edison

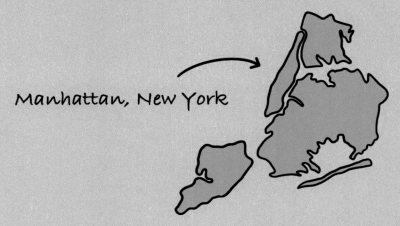

Manhattan, New York

Nikola arrived in New York in 1884 and was hired as an engineer at Thomas Edison's Manhattan headquarters.

Nikola worked there for a year and impressed Thomas with his diligence and ingenuity.

Nikola Tesla

Thomas Edison

Nikola Tesla and Thomas Edison parted ways because he refused to pay Nikola the money he owed him for a solution for an improved design for his DC dynamos.

They also parted ways due to a conflicting business-scientific relationship. Thomas was championing direct current as opposed to Nikola's alternating current, in which was later to be known as the War of Currents.

Inventions

Nikola Tesla developed and invented many important inventions throughout his lifetime, but most of these inventions were officially patented by other inventors.

He had over 1000 patents for his inventions.

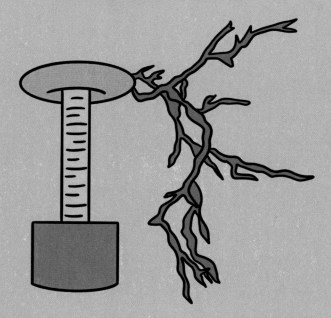

The Tesla Coil was invented in 1891 and it's widely used in radio technology. Its patent number is 454,622.

Nikola invented the Tesla Coil with the intentions of transmitting electricity through the air.

The Tesla Coil was one of Nikola's most famous inventions.

It is a high-frequency air-core transformer and the voltages can get to be well above 1,000,000 volts. Nikola himself got arcs up to 100,000,000 volts, but it has not been duplicated by anyone else.

Tesla Coils are known to create extremely powerful electrical fields.

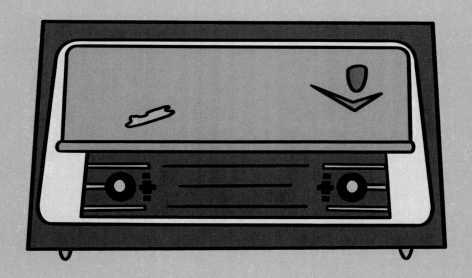

The radio was invented in 1898 and was patented as a radio controlled robot-boat.

He used this boat which was controlled by radio waves in the Electrical Exhibition in 1898, in Madison Square Garden.

Nikola's robot-boat was constructed with an antenna, which transmitted the radio waves.

The radio waves were received by a radio sensitive device called coherer, which transmitted the radio waves into mechanical movements of the propellers on the boat.

Guglielmo Marconi claimed all the first patents for the radio, something originally invented by Tesla.

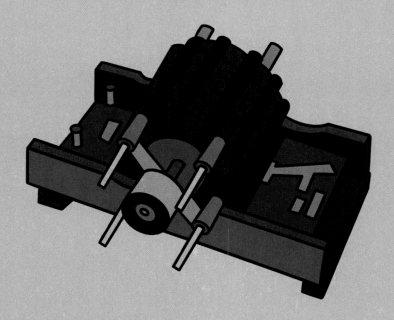

In 1887, Nikola invented the first alternating current (AC) motor.

The Tesla AC was used for distributing power over a distance because of its ease to change voltages using a transformer.

Nikola Tesla partnered with George Westinghouse to develop the AC technology and together they made the first power generating system on Niagara Falls in 1893.

The Tesla AC converted electrical energy into mechanical energy with the use of the electro magnecitic induction. This was turning current into motion, which had never been done more efficiently before.

Predictions

Nikola Tesla had made many predictions to what he had envisioned the future to look like.

Most of Nikola's predictions had already come true and some might in the near future.

Nikola Tesla predicted a wireless device that would incorporate video and telephone technology like a smartphone.

He also envisioned that it would work over a network very much like the Internet.

In 1926, Nikola Tesla described his prediction.

He said, "We shall be able to communicate with one another instantly, irrespective of distance. Not only this, but through television and telephony we shall see and hear one another as perfectly as though we were face to face, despite intervening distances of thousands of miles and a man will be able to carry one in his vest pocket."

Nikola Tesla was obsessed
with wireless technology
and was also a big
proponent of wireless
transmission.

He was able to envision wi-
fi and how wireless devices
would work.

In the late 1800's, Nikola described his prediction.

He said, "A present wireless receiving apparatus will be scrapped for much simpler machines; and all forms of interference will be eliminated, so that transmitters and receivers may be operated without interference. The problems of heat, light and household mechanics will be freed from all labor through beneficent wireless power."

Nikola Tesla imagined a machine that would allow one to project a mental image in real life and play back your thoughts.

Nikola came up with this idea in 1893, while he was working on experiments.

Decades later Nikola described his prediction.

He said, "I was convinced that a definite image formed in thought must, by reflex action, produce a corresponding image on the retina, which might be read by suitable apparatus. If this can be done successfully, then the objects imagined by a person would be clearly reflected on the screen and our minds would then, indeed, be like open books."

Achievements

Nikola Tesla has made many achievements throughout his life and has impacted the world in so many ways.

He is a scientist and an inventor who is also known as "The Genius Who Lit the World."

Some of Nikola Tesla's main achievements are:

• Rotating Magnetic Field (which was discovered 1882 in Budapest, Hungary)
• Alternating Current (which is lighting the whole world today)
• AC Motor (one of the ten greatest discoveries of all time)
• Tesla Coil
• Tesla Unit T $=W/m^2$ (all MRI machines are calibrated in Tesla Units)

- Niagara Falls Power Plant (built in 1885)
- Radio
- Colorado Springs Laboratory (in 1899)
- Neon Lights
- Wardenclyffe Tower (Tesla's Wireless World System, built in 1901-1905)
- Robotics
- Transmission of Electrical Energy without wires
- Free Energy
- Use of Ionosphere for scientific purposes
- X-rays

Awards

Nikola had four awards.

He was awarded with The Elliott Cresson Medal, The IEEE Edison Medal, The John Scott Legacy Medal and Premium, and The Royal Order of the Yugoslav Crown.

Elliott Cresson Medal was awarded in 1894.

IEEE Edison Medal was awarded in 1916.

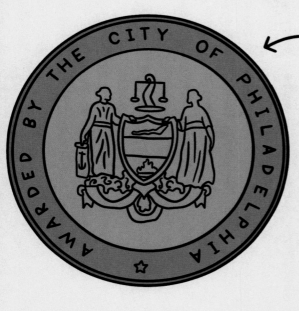

John Scott Legacy Medal and Premium was awarded in 1934.

Order of the Yugoslav Crown was awarded in 1931.

Death Ray

Nikola Tesla was working on particle accelerators which aimed to send a concentrated beam of energy in a vertical line without diffusion.

It is unknown if he was successful in building it.

In 1934, Nikola presented an amazing new device to the U.S. military.

The device was the first particle beam projector in history to be taken seriously. It was also the first to be deemed realistic and achievable.

Nikola had stated that this device could attack a target 200 miles away, leveling millions of soldiers or a fleet of 10,000 aircrafts.

Before his death, Nikola claimed to had successfully develop the death ray, which he called the Teleforce.

Later, he also described the abilities of the Teleforce.

He said, "It would destroy anything approaching within 200 miles and will provide a wall of power in order to make any country, large or small, impregnable against armies, airplanes, and other means for attack."

"This invention of mine does not contemplate the use of any so-called 'death rays'. Rays are not applicable because they cannot be produced in requisite quantities and diminish rapidly in intensity with distance. All the energy of New York City (approximately two million horsepower) transformed into rays and projected twenty miles, could not kill a human being, because, according to a well known law of physics, it would disperse to such an extent as to be ineffectual. My apparatus projects particles which may be relatively large or of microscopic dimensions, enabling us to convey to a small area at a great distance trillions of times more energy than is possible with rays of any kind. Many thousands of horsepower can thus be transmitted by a stream thinner than a hair, so that nothing can resist."

Missing Files

Nikola Tesla was found dead on January 7, 1943 in his hotel room in New York.

The US government's Office of Alien Property took the majority of the documents relating to his inventions, ideas, and works.

After Nikola's death, his belongings and documents were given a thorough examination by a group of FBI agents and John Trump who was the head of research at MIT, in the high voltage research lab.

John Trump

After years of questions, the FBI finally declassified about 250 pages of Nikola Tesla related documents under the Freedom of Information Act in 2016.

In 2018, the FBI followed up with two additional releases.

Since the publications of these documents, many questions still remain unanswered and some of his files are still missing.

The Truth

A declassified FBI document states that Nikola Tesla invented a radio type machine in 1938. It was used for interplanetary communication.

This machine was not built until after his death.

This radio type machine was placed in operation in 1950.

Since 1950, Nikola Tesla's engineers have been in close contact with space ships.

The space people have visited them many times, and have told them Nikola Tesla was a Venusian.

He was brought to this planet as a baby in 1856, and was left with Mr. and Mrs. Tesla.

He stayed in a remote mountain province, which is now known as Yogoslavia.

This information can be found on vault.fbi.gov under the name Nikola Tesla Part 03 of 03. This document was released on September 21st 2016 and contains 64 pages.

The document title is called "Interplanetary Sessions Newsletter" and was written on June 14, 1957.

Wrap Up

Nikola Tesla was incredibly intelligent and was between 300 to a 1,000 years ahead of his time.

The world would be about half a century behind where we are today if it wasn't for Nikola Tesla.

In 1905, Nikola Tesla had a patent called "The art of transmitting electrical energy through the natural medium."

This was based on his thoughts that the Earth was an electrical generator that could supply an unlimited amount of electricity.

Nikola Tesla is the genius who harnessed lightning and envisioned new technologies far before their time.

Nikola believed that there was alien life in the cosmos.

In 1900, he was working at his Colorado Springs laboratory and announced that he intercepted extra terrestrial radio signals.

Even though he is absent from our history books, he is one of the greatest scientific minds the world has ever known and created the foundation for today's technology and lifestyle.

"If you want to find the
secrets of the universe,
think in terms of energy,
frequency, and vibration."
~ Nikola Tesla

The End!

remember to:

BELIEVE
DREAM
ACHIEVE

MORE Bearific® books on bearific.com

Katelyn Lonas

Katelyn is a 15 year old who resides in Southern California. Katelyn loves to encourage others to always believe in themselves and chase after their dreams! She started writing and illustrating her first book at age 9 and then published 49 more books. She hopes you enjoy reading this book and be ready for more books to come!

-Katelyn

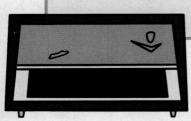

Made in the USA
Las Vegas, NV
10 January 2025

16235168R00040